This Belongs To:

_____

Prayer Warrior

Sermon And Bible Study

Prayer Notes For The Soul

Published By: Tina's Gifts & More
ISBN: 978-1-965870-00-6
Edition: 2nd Edition
Printed in United States Of America

Church Events

Title: _____

Date: _____

Time: _____

Place: _____

Title: _____

Date: _____

Time: _____

Place: _____

Title: _____

Date: _____

Time: _____

Place: _____

Church Events

Title: _____

Date: _____

Time: _____

Place: _____

Title: _____

Date: _____

Time: _____

Place: _____

Title: _____

Date: _____

Time: _____

Place: _____

Church Events

Title: _____
Date: _____
Time: _____
Place: _____

Title: _____
Date: _____
Time: _____
Place: _____

Title: _____
Date: _____
Time: _____
Place: _____

Church Events

Title: _____

Date: _____

Time: _____

Place: _____

Title: _____

Date: _____

Time: _____

Place: _____

Title: _____

Date: _____

Time: _____

Place: _____

Confess your faults one to another, and pray one for another, that ye may be healed. The effectual fervent prayer of a righteous man availeth much.

~~ James 5:16 KJV~~

 # Prayer List

Prayer   Answered

 # Prayer List

Prayer   Answered

Sermon/Bible Study

&

Reflections

Now faith is the substance of things hoped for, the evidence of things not seen.
~~ Hebrews 11:1 KJV~~

SERMON/BIBLE STUDY

DATE: _____

PREACHER: _____

SCRIPTURE: _____

Key Verses:

Title: _____

Notes: _____
_____
_____
_____
_____
_____
_____
_____
_____
_____
_____
_____

SERMON/BIBLE STUDY

Key Verses:

Reflections:

SERMON/BIBLE STUDY

DATE: _____

PREACHER: _____

SCRIPTURE: _____

Key Verses:

Title: _____

Notes: _____

SERMON/BIBLE STUDY

Reflections:

SERMON/BIBLE STUDY

DATE: _____

PREACHER: _____

SCRIPTURE: _____

Key Verses:

Title: _____

Notes: _____

SERMON/BIBLE STUDY

Key Verses:

Reflections:

SERMON/BIBLE STUDY

DATE: _____

PREACHER: _____

SCRIPTURE: _____

Key Verses:

Title: _____

Notes:

_____
_____
_____
_____
_____
_____
_____
_____
_____
_____
_____
_____
_____

SERMON/BIBLE STUDY

Key Verses:

Reflections:

SERMON/BIBLE STUDY

DATE: _____

PREACHER: _____

SCRIPTURE: _____

Key Verses:

Title: _____

Notes: _____

SERMON/BIBLE STUDY

Key Verses:

Reflections:

SERMON/BIBLE STUDY

DATE: _____

PREACHER: _____

SCRIPTURE: _____

Key Verses:

Title: _____

Notes: _____

_____

_____

_____

_____

_____

_____

_____

_____

_____

_____

_____

SERMON/BIBLE STUDY

Key Verses:

Reflections:

SERMON/BIBLE STUDY

DATE: _____

PREACHER: _____

SCRIPTURE: _____

Key Verses:

Title: _____

Notes: _____

_____

_____

_____

_____

_____

_____

_____

_____

_____

_____

_____

_____

SERMON/BIBLE STUDY

Reflections:

SERMON/BIBLE STUDY

DATE: _____

PREACHER: _____

SCRIPTURE: _____

Key Verses:

Title: _____

Notes: _____

SERMON/BIBLE STUDY

Key Verses:

Reflections:

SERMON/BIBLE STUDY

DATE: _____

PREACHER: _____

SCRIPTURE: _____

Key Verses:

Title: _____

Notes: _____

_____

_____

_____

_____

_____

_____

_____

_____

_____

_____

_____

_____

_____

_____

SERMON/BIBLE STUDY

_____

_____

_____

_____

_____

Key Verses:

_____

_____

_____

_____

_____

_____

_____

_____

_____

_____

_____

Reflections: _____

_____

_____

_____

SERMON/BIBLE STUDY

DATE: _____

PREACHER: _____

SCRIPTURE: _____

Key Verses:

Title: _____

Notes: _____

SERMON/BIBLE STUDY

Key Verses:

Reflections:

SERMON/BIBLE STUDY

DATE: _____

Key Verses:

PREACHER: _____

_____

SCRIPTURE: _____

_____

Title: _____

Notes: _____

_____

_____

_____

_____

_____

_____

_____

_____

_____

_____

_____

SERMON/BIBLE STUDY

Key Verses:

Reflections:

SERMON/BIBLE STUDY

DATE: _____

PREACHER: _____

SCRIPTURE: _____

Key Verses:

Title: _____

Notes: _____

_____

_____

_____

_____

_____

_____

_____

_____

_____

_____

_____

_____

SERMON/BIBLE STUDY

Key Verses:

Reflections:

SERMON/BIBLE STUDY

DATE: _____

PREACHER: _____

SCRIPTURE: _____

Key Verses:

Title: _____

Notes: _____

_____

_____

_____

_____

_____

_____

_____

_____

_____

_____

_____

_____

_____

SERMON/BIBLE STUDY

Key Verses:

Reflections:

SERMON/BIBLE STUDY

DATE: _____

PREACHER: _____

SCRIPTURE: _____

Key Verses:

Title: _____

Notes: _____

_____

_____

_____

_____

_____

_____

_____

_____

_____

_____

_____

_____

SERMON/BIBLE STUDY

Key Verses:

Reflections:

SERMON/BIBLE STUDY

DATE: _____

PREACHER: _____

_____

SCRIPTURE: _____

_____

Key Verses:

Title: _____

Notes: _____

_____

_____

_____

_____

_____

_____

_____

_____

_____

_____

_____

SERMON/BIBLE STUDY

Key Verses:

Reflections:

SERMON/BIBLE STUDY

DATE: _____

PREACHER: _____

SCRIPTURE: _____

Key Verses:

Title: _____

Notes:

_____

_____

_____

_____

_____

_____

_____

_____

_____

_____

_____

_____

SERMON/BIBLE STUDY

_____

_____

_____

_____

_____

_____

Key Verses:

_____

_____

_____

_____

_____

_____

_____

_____

_____

_____

_____

_____

Reflections: _____

_____

_____

_____

SERMON/BIBLE STUDY

DATE: _____

PREACHER: _____

SCRIPTURE: _____

Key Verses:

Title: _____

Notes: _____

_____

_____

_____

_____

_____

_____

_____

_____

_____

_____

_____

_____

SERMON/BIBLE STUDY

Key Verses:

Reflections:

SERMON/BIBLE STUDY

DATE: _____

PREACHER: _____

SCRIPTURE: _____

Key Verses:

Title: _____

Notes: _____

SERMON/BIBLE STUDY

Key Verses:

Reflections:

SERMON/BIBLE STUDY

DATE: _____

PREACHER: _____

SCRIPTURE: _____

Key Verses:

Title: _____

Notes: _____

SERMON/BIBLE STUDY

Key Verses:

Reflections:

SERMON/BIBLE STUDY

DATE: _____

PREACHER: _____

SCRIPTURE: _____

Key Verses:

Title: _____

Notes: _____

_____

_____

_____

_____

_____

_____

_____

_____

_____

_____

_____

_____

_____

SERMON/BIBLE STUDY

Key Verses:

Reflections:

SERMON/BIBLE STUDY

DATE: _____

PREACHER: _____

SCRIPTURE: _____

Key Verses:

Title: _____

Notes: _____

SERMON/BIBLE STUDY

Key Verses:

Reflections:

SERMON/BIBLE STUDY

DATE: _____

PREACHER: _____

SCRIPTURE: _____

Key Verses:

Title: _____

Notes:

_____
_____
_____
_____
_____
_____
_____
_____
_____
_____
_____
_____

SERMON/BIBLE STUDY

Key Verses:

Reflections:

SERMON/BIBLE STUDY

DATE: _____

PREACHER: _____

SCRIPTURE: _____

Key Verses:

Title: _____

Notes:

SERMON/BIBLE STUDY

Key Verses:

Reflections:

SERMON/BIBLE STUDY

DATE: _____

Key Verses:

PREACHER: _____

SCRIPTURE: _____

Title: _____

Notes: _____

_____

_____

_____

_____

_____

_____

_____

_____

_____

_____

_____

_____

_____

SERMON/BIBLE STUDY

Key Verses:

Reflections:

SERMON/BIBLE STUDY

DATE: _____

PREACHER: _____

SCRIPTURE: _____

Key Verses:

Title: _____

Notes:
_____
_____
_____
_____
_____
_____
_____
_____
_____
_____
_____
_____
_____
_____

SERMON/BIBLE STUDY

Key Verses:

Reflections:

SERMON/BIBLE STUDY

DATE: _____

PREACHER: _____
_____

SCRIPTURE: _____
_____

Key Verses:

Title: _____

_____

Notes: _____

_____

_____

_____

_____

_____

_____

_____

_____

_____

_____

_____

_____

SERMON/BIBLE STUDY

Key Verses:

Reflections:

SERMON/BIBLE STUDY

DATE: _____

Key Verses:

PREACHER: _____

SCRIPTURE: _____

Title: _____

Notes: _____

_____

_____

_____

_____

_____

_____

_____

_____

_____

_____

_____

_____

SERMON/BIBLE STUDY

Key Verses:

Reflections:

SERMON/BIBLE STUDY

DATE: _____

PREACHER: _____

SCRIPTURE: _____

Key Verses:

Title: _____

Notes: _____

_____

_____

_____

_____

_____

_____

_____

_____

_____

_____

_____

_____

SERMON/BIBLE STUDY

Key Verses:

Reflections:

SERMON/BIBLE STUDY

DATE: _____

PREACHER: _____

SCRIPTURE: _____

Key Verses:

Title: _____

Notes: _____
_____
_____
_____
_____
_____
_____
_____
_____
_____
_____
_____
_____
_____

SERMON/BIBLE STUDY

Key Verses:

Reflections:

SERMON/BIBLE STUDY

DATE: _____

PREACHER: _____

_____

SCRIPTURE: _____

_____

Key Verses:

Title: _____

Notes: _____

_____

_____

_____

_____

_____

_____

_____

_____

_____

_____

_____

_____

SERMON/BIBLE STUDY

Key Verses:

Reflections:

SERMON/BIBLE STUDY

DATE: _____

PREACHER: _____

SCRIPTURE: _____

Key Verses:

Title: _____

Notes: _____
_____
_____
_____
_____
_____
_____
_____
_____
_____
_____
_____
_____
_____
_____

SERMON/BIBLE STUDY

Key Verses:

Reflections:

SERMON/BIBLE STUDY

DATE: _____

PREACHER: _____

SCRIPTURE: _____

Key Verses:

Title: _____

Notes:
_____
_____
_____
_____
_____
_____
_____
_____
_____
_____
_____
_____
_____
_____

SERMON/BIBLE STUDY

Key Verses:

Reflections:

SERMON/BIBLE STUDY

DATE: _____

PREACHER: _____

SCRIPTURE: _____

Key Verses:

Title: _____

Notes: _____

_____

_____

_____

_____

_____

_____

_____

_____

_____

_____

_____

_____

SERMON/BIBLE STUDY

Key Verses:

Reflections:

SERMON/BIBLE STUDY

DATE: _____

PREACHER: _____

SCRIPTURE: _____

Key Verses:

Title: _____

Notes:
_____
_____
_____
_____
_____
_____
_____
_____
_____
_____
_____
_____

SERMON/BIBLE STUDY

_____

_____

_____

_____

_____

Key Verses:

_____

_____

_____

_____

_____

_____

_____

_____

_____

_____

_____

Reflections: _____

_____

_____

_____

SERMON/BIBLE STUDY

DATE: _____

PREACHER: _____

SCRIPTURE: _____

Key Verses:

Title: _____

Notes: _____

_____

_____

_____

_____

_____

_____

_____

_____

_____

_____

_____

SERMON/BIBLE STUDY

Key Verses:

Reflections:

SERMON/BIBLE STUDY

DATE: _____

PREACHER: _____
_____

SCRIPTURE: _____
_____

Key Verses:

Title: _____
_____

Notes: _____
_____
_____
_____
_____
_____
_____
_____
_____
_____
_____
_____
_____

SERMON/BIBLE STUDY

_____

_____

_____

_____

_____

_____

Key Verses:

_____

_____

_____

_____

_____

_____

_____

_____

_____

_____

_____

Reflections: _____

_____

_____

_____

SERMON/BIBLE STUDY

DATE: _____

PREACHER: _____

SCRIPTURE: _____

Key Verses:

Title: _____

Notes: _____

SERMON/BIBLE STUDY

Key Verses:

Reflections:

SERMON/BIBLE STUDY

DATE: _____

PREACHER: _____

SCRIPTURE: _____

Key Verses:

Title: _____

Notes: _____

_____

_____

_____

_____

_____

_____

_____

_____

_____

_____

_____

_____

SERMON/BIBLE STUDY

Key Verses:

Reflections:

SERMON/BIBLE STUDY

DATE: _____

PREACHER: _____

SCRIPTURE: _____

Key Verses:

Title: _____

Notes: _____

SERMON/BIBLE STUDY

Key Verses:

Reflections:

SERMON/BIBLE STUDY

DATE: _____

Key Verses:

PREACHER: _____

_____

SCRIPTURE: _____

_____

Title: _____

_____

Notes: _____

_____

_____

_____

_____

_____

_____

_____

_____

_____

_____

_____

_____

_____

SERMON/BIBLE STUDY

Key Verses:

Reflections:

SERMON/BIBLE STUDY

DATE: _____

PREACHER: _____

_____

SCRIPTURE: _____

_____

Key Verses:

Title: _____

Notes:

SERMON/BIBLE STUDY

Key Verses:

Reflections:

SERMON/BIBLE STUDY

DATE: _____

PREACHER: _____

SCRIPTURE: _____

Key Verses:

Title: _____

Notes: _____

_____

_____

_____

_____

_____

_____

_____

_____

_____

_____

_____

_____

SERMON/BIBLE STUDY

Key Verses:

Reflections:

SERMON/BIBLE STUDY

DATE: _____

PREACHER: _____

SCRIPTURE: _____

Key Verses:

Title: _____

Notes: _____

_____

_____

_____

_____

_____

_____

_____

_____

_____

_____

_____

_____

_____

SERMON/BIBLE STUDY

Key Verses:

Reflections:

SERMON/BIBLE STUDY

DATE: _____

PREACHER: _____

SCRIPTURE: _____

Key Verses:

Title: _____

Notes: _____

SERMON/BIBLE STUDY

Key Verses:

_____

Reflections:

SERMON/BIBLE STUDY

DATE: _____

Key Verses:

PREACHER: _____

SCRIPTURE: _____

Title: _____

Notes: _____

SERMON/BIBLE STUDY

Key Verses:

_____

_____

_____

_____

_____

_____

_____

_____

_____

_____

_____

_____

_____

_____

_____

_____

Reflections: _____

_____

_____

_____

SERMON/BIBLE STUDY

DATE: _____

PREACHER: _____

SCRIPTURE: _____

_____

Key Verses:

Title: _____

_____

Notes: _____

_____

_____

_____

_____

_____

_____

_____

_____

_____

_____

_____

_____

_____

SERMON/BIBLE STUDY

Key Verses:

Reflections:

SERMON/BIBLE STUDY

DATE: _____

PREACHER: _____

SCRIPTURE: _____

Key Verses:

Title: _____

Notes: _____

SERMON/BIBLE STUDY

Key Verses:

Reflections:

SERMON/BIBLE STUDY

DATE: _____

PREACHER: _____

SCRIPTURE: _____

Key Verses:

Title: _____

Notes: _____

SERMON/BIBLE STUDY

Key Verses:

Reflections:

SERMON/BIBLE STUDY

DATE: _____

PREACHER: _____

SCRIPTURE: _____

Key Verses:

Title: _____

Notes:

SERMON/BIBLE STUDY

Key Verses:

Reflections:

SERMON/BIBLE STUDY

DATE: _____

PREACHER: _____

_____

SCRIPTURE: _____

_____

Key Verses:

Title: _____

_____

Notes: _____

_____

_____

_____

_____

_____

_____

_____

_____

_____

_____

_____

_____

_____

SERMON/BIBLE STUDY

Key Verses:

Reflections:

SERMON/BIBLE STUDY

DATE: _____

PREACHER: _____

SCRIPTURE: _____

Key Verses:

Title: _____

Notes: _____

SERMON/BIBLE STUDY

Key Verses:

Reflections:

SERMON/BIBLE STUDY

DATE: _____

PREACHER: _____

_____

SCRIPTURE: _____

_____

Key Verses:

Title: _____

_____

Notes: _____

_____

_____

_____

_____

_____

_____

_____

_____

_____

_____

_____

_____

SERMON/BIBLE STUDY

Key Verses:

Reflections:

SERMON/BIBLE STUDY

DATE: _____

PREACHER: _____

SCRIPTURE: _____

Key Verses:

Title: _____

Notes: _____

SERMON/BIBLE STUDY

Key Verses:

Reflections:

SERMON/BIBLE STUDY

DATE: _____

PREACHER: _____

SCRIPTURE: _____

Key Verses:

Title: _____

Notes: _____

SERMON/BIBLE STUDY

Key Verses:

Reflections:

SERMON/BIBLE STUDY

DATE: _____

PREACHER: _____

SCRIPTURE: _____

Key Verses:

Title: _____

Notes: _____

_____

_____

_____

_____

_____

_____

_____

_____

_____

_____

_____

_____

_____

SERMON/BIBLE STUDY

Key Verses:

Reflections:

SERMON/BIBLE STUDY

DATE: _____

PREACHER: _____

SCRIPTURE: _____

Key Verses:

Title: _____

Notes: _____

_____

_____

_____

_____

_____

_____

_____

_____

_____

_____

_____

_____

_____

SERMON/BIBLE STUDY

Key Verses:

Reflections:

SERMON/BIBLE STUDY

DATE: _____

PREACHER: _____

SCRIPTURE: _____

Key Verses:

Title: _____

Notes: _____

_____

_____

_____

_____

_____

_____

_____

_____

_____

_____

_____

_____

SERMON/BIBLE STUDY

Key Verses:

Reflections:

SERMON/BIBLE STUDY

DATE: _____

PREACHER: _____

SCRIPTURE: _____

Key Verses:

Title: _____

Notes: _____

SERMON/BIBLE STUDY

_____

_____

_____

_____

_____

_____

Key Verses:

_____

_____

_____

_____

_____

_____

_____

_____

_____

_____

Reflections: _____

_____

_____

_____

SERMON/BIBLE STUDY

DATE: _____

PREACHER: _____

SCRIPTURE: _____

Key Verses:

Title: _____

Notes: _____

_____

_____

_____

_____

_____

_____

_____

_____

_____

_____

_____

_____

SERMON/BIBLE STUDY

Key Verses:

Reflections:

SERMON/BIBLE STUDY

DATE: _____

PREACHER: _____

SCRIPTURE: _____

Key Verses:

Title: _____

Notes: _____

SERMON/BIBLE STUDY

Key Verses:

Reflections:

SERMON/BIBLE STUDY

DATE: _____

PREACHER: _____

SCRIPTURE: _____

Key Verses:

Title: _____

Notes: _____

SERMON/BIBLE STUDY

_____

_____

_____

_____

_____

_____

Key Verses:

_____

_____

_____

_____

_____

_____

_____

_____

_____

_____

_____

Reflections: _____

_____

_____

_____

SERMON/BIBLE STUDY

DATE: _____

PREACHER: _____

SCRIPTURE: _____

Key Verses:

Title: _____

Notes:
_____
_____
_____
_____
_____
_____
_____
_____
_____
_____
_____
_____
_____

SERMON/BIBLE STUDY

Key Verses:

Reflections:

SERMON/BIBLE STUDY

DATE: _____

PREACHER: _____

SCRIPTURE: _____

Key Verses:

Title: _____

Notes: _____

_____

_____

_____

_____

_____

_____

_____

_____

_____

_____

_____

SERMON/BIBLE STUDY

Key Verses:

Reflections:

SERMON/BIBLE STUDY

DATE: _____

PREACHER: _____

SCRIPTURE: _____

Key Verses:

Title: _____

_____

Notes: _____

_____

_____

_____

_____

_____

_____

_____

_____

_____

_____

_____

_____

SERMON/BIBLE STUDY

Key Verses:

Reflections:

SERMON/BIBLE STUDY

DATE: _____

Key Verses:

PREACHER: _____
_____

SCRIPTURE: _____
_____

Title: _____

Notes: _____
_____
_____
_____
_____
_____
_____
_____
_____
_____
_____
_____
_____
_____

SERMON/BIBLE STUDY

Key Verses:

Reflections:

SERMON/BIBLE STUDY

DATE: _____

PREACHER: _____

SCRIPTURE: _____

Key Verses:

Title: _____

Notes: _____

_____

_____

_____

_____

_____

_____

_____

_____

_____

_____

_____

SERMON/BIBLE STUDY

Key Verses:

Reflections:

SERMON/BIBLE STUDY

DATE: _____

PREACHER: _____

SCRIPTURE: _____

Key Verses:

Title: _____

Notes: _____

SERMON/BIBLE STUDY

Key Verses:

Reflections:

SERMON/BIBLE STUDY

DATE: _____

PREACHER: _____

SCRIPTURE: _____

Key Verses:

Title: _____

Notes: _____

_____

_____

_____

_____

_____

_____

_____

_____

_____

_____

_____

_____

_____

_____

SERMON/BIBLE STUDY

_____

_____

_____

_____

_____

_____

Key Verses:

_____

_____

_____

_____

_____

_____

_____

_____

_____

_____

Reflections: _____

_____

_____

_____

SERMON/BIBLE STUDY

DATE: _____

PREACHER: _____

SCRIPTURE: _____

Key Verses:

Title: _____

Notes: _____

_____

_____

_____

_____

_____

_____

_____

_____

_____

_____

_____

SERMON/BIBLE STUDY

Key Verses:

Reflections:

SERMON/BIBLE STUDY

DATE: _____

PREACHER: _____

SCRIPTURE: _____

Key Verses:

Title: _____

Notes: _____

SERMON/BIBLE STUDY

Key Verses:

Reflections:

SERMON/BIBLE STUDY

DATE: _____

PREACHER: _____

SCRIPTURE: _____

Key Verses:

Title: _____

Notes: _____

_____

_____

_____

_____

_____

_____

_____

_____

_____

_____

_____

_____

_____

_____

SERMON/BIBLE STUDY

Key Verses:

Reflections:

SERMON/BIBLE STUDY

DATE: _____

PREACHER: _____

SCRIPTURE: _____

Key Verses:

Title: _____

Notes: _____

_____

_____

_____

_____

_____

_____

_____

_____

_____

_____

_____

_____

_____

SERMON/BIBLE STUDY

Key Verses:

_____

Reflections: _____

SERMON/BIBLE STUDY

DATE: _____

PREACHER: _____

SCRIPTURE: _____

Key Verses:

Title: _____

Notes: _____

SERMON/BIBLE STUDY

Key Verses:

Reflections:

SERMON/BIBLE STUDY

DATE: _____

Key Verses:

PREACHER: _____

SCRIPTURE: _____

Title: _____

Notes: _____

SERMON/BIBLE STUDY

Key Verses:

Reflections:

SERMON/BIBLE STUDY

DATE: _____

Key Verses:

PREACHER: _____

SCRIPTURE: _____

Title: _____

Notes: _____

_____

_____

_____

_____

_____

_____

_____

_____

_____

_____

_____

_____

_____

SERMON/BIBLE STUDY

Key Verses:

_____

Reflections: _____

SERMON/BIBLE STUDY

DATE: _____

PREACHER: _____

SCRIPTURE: _____

Key Verses:

Title: _____

Notes: _____

SERMON/BIBLE STUDY

Key Verses:

Reflections:

SERMON/BIBLE STUDY

DATE: _____

PREACHER: _____

_____

SCRIPTURE: _____

_____

Key Verses:

Title: _____

Notes: _____

_____

_____

_____

_____

_____

_____

_____

_____

_____

_____

_____

_____

_____

SERMON/BIBLE STUDY

Key Verses:

Reflections:

SERMON/BIBLE STUDY

DATE: _____

Key Verses:

PREACHER: _____

SCRIPTURE: _____

Title: _____

Notes: _____

_____

_____

_____

_____

_____

_____

_____

_____

_____

_____

_____

_____

SERMON/BIBLE STUDY

Key Verses:

Reflections:

SERMON/BIBLE STUDY

DATE: _____

PREACHER: _____

SCRIPTURE: _____

Key Verses:

Title: _____

Notes: _____

SERMON/BIBLE STUDY

Key Verses:

Reflections:

SERMON/BIBLE STUDY

DATE: _____

PREACHER: _____

_____
SCRIPTURE: _____

_____

Key Verses:

Title: _____

_____

Notes: _____

_____

_____

_____

_____

_____

_____

_____

_____

_____

_____

_____

SERMON/BIBLE STUDY

Key Verses:

Reflections:

SERMON/BIBLE STUDY

DATE: _____

Key Verses:

PREACHER: _____

SCRIPTURE: _____

Title: _____

Notes: _____

SERMON/BIBLE STUDY

Key Verses:

Reflections:

SERMON/BIBLE STUDY

DATE: _____

PREACHER: _____

SCRIPTURE: _____

Key Verses:

Title: _____

Notes: _____

SERMON/BIBLE STUDY

Key Verses:

Reflections:

SERMON/BIBLE STUDY

DATE: _____

PREACHER: _____

SCRIPTURE: _____

Key Verses:

Title: _____

Notes: _____

_____

_____

_____

_____

_____

_____

_____

_____

_____

_____

_____

_____

_____

SERMON/BIBLE STUDY

Key Verses:

_____

Reflections:

SERMON/BIBLE STUDY

DATE: _____

Key Verses:

PREACHER: _____

SCRIPTURE: _____

Title: _____

Notes: _____
_____
_____
_____
_____
_____
_____
_____
_____
_____
_____
_____
_____

SERMON/BIBLE STUDY

Key Verses:

Reflections:

SERMON/BIBLE STUDY

DATE: _____

PREACHER: _____

SCRIPTURE: _____

Key Verses:

Title: _____

Notes: _____
_____
_____
_____
_____
_____
_____
_____
_____
_____
_____
_____
_____

SERMON/BIBLE STUDY

_____

_____

_____

_____

_____

_____

Key Verses:

_____

_____

_____

_____

_____

_____

_____

_____

_____

_____

_____

Reflections: _____

_____

_____

_____

SERMON/BIBLE STUDY

DATE: _____

PREACHER: _____

SCRIPTURE: _____

Key Verses:

Title: _____

Notes: _____
_____
_____
_____
_____
_____
_____
_____
_____
_____
_____
_____
_____

SERMON/BIBLE STUDY

Key Verses:

Reflections:

SERMON/BIBLE STUDY

DATE: _____

PREACHER: _____

SCRIPTURE: _____

Key Verses:

Title: _____

Notes: _____

SERMON/BIBLE STUDY

Key Verses:

_____

_____

_____

_____

_____

_____

_____

_____

_____

_____

_____

_____

_____

_____

_____

Reflections: _____

_____

_____

_____

SERMON/BIBLE STUDY

DATE: _____

PREACHER: _____

SCRIPTURE: _____

Key Verses:

Title: _____

Notes: _____

SERMON/BIBLE STUDY

Key Verses:

Reflections:

SERMON/BIBLE STUDY

DATE: _____

PREACHER: _____

SCRIPTURE: _____

Key Verses:

Title: _____

Notes: _____

_____

_____

_____

_____

_____

_____

_____

_____

_____

_____

_____

_____

_____

SERMON/BIBLE STUDY

Key Verses:

Reflections:

SERMON/BIBLE STUDY

DATE: _____

Key Verses:

PREACHER: _____

SCRIPTURE: _____

Title: _____

Notes: _____

SERMON/BIBLE STUDY

Key Verses:

Reflections:

SERMON/BIBLE STUDY

DATE: _____

PREACHER: _____

SCRIPTURE: _____

Key Verses:

Title: _____

Notes: _____
_____
_____
_____
_____
_____
_____
_____
_____
_____
_____
_____
_____

SERMON/BIBLE STUDY

Key Verses:

Reflections:

SERMON/BIBLE STUDY

DATE: _____

PREACHER: _____

SCRIPTURE: _____

Key Verses:

Title: _____

Notes:
_____
_____
_____
_____
_____
_____
_____
_____
_____
_____
_____
_____
_____

SERMON/BIBLE STUDY

Key Verses:

Reflections:

SERMON/BIBLE STUDY

DATE: _____

PREACHER: _____

SCRIPTURE: _____

Key Verses:

Title: _____

Notes: _____

_____

_____

_____

_____

_____

_____

_____

_____

_____

_____

_____

_____

SERMON/BIBLE STUDY

Key Verses:

Reflections:

SERMON/BIBLE STUDY

DATE: _____

PREACHER: _____

SCRIPTURE: _____

Key Verses:

Title: _____

Notes: _____

SERMON/BIBLE STUDY

Key Verses:

Reflections:

SERMON/BIBLE STUDY

DATE: _____

PREACHER: _____

SCRIPTURE: _____

Key Verses:

Title: _____

Notes: _____

SERMON/BIBLE STUDY

Key Verses:

Reflections:

SERMON/BIBLE STUDY

DATE: _____

PREACHER: _____

SCRIPTURE: _____

Key Verses:

Title: _____

Notes: _____

SERMON/BIBLE STUDY

Key Verses:

Reflections:

SERMON/BIBLE STUDY

DATE: _____

PREACHER: _____

SCRIPTURE: _____

Key Verses:

Title: _____

Notes: _____

SERMON/BIBLE STUDY

Key Verses:

_____

Reflections: _____

SERMON/BIBLE STUDY

DATE: _____

PREACHER: _____

SCRIPTURE: _____

Key Verses:

Title: _____

Notes: _____

_____

_____

_____

_____

_____

_____

_____

_____

_____

_____

_____

_____

_____

SERMON/BIBLE STUDY

Key Verses:

Reflections:

SERMON/BIBLE STUDY

DATE: _____

PREACHER: _____

SCRIPTURE: _____

Key Verses:

Title: _____

Notes: _____

_____

_____

_____

_____

_____

_____

_____

_____

_____

_____

_____

_____

SERMON/BIBLE STUDY

Key Verses:

Reflections:

SERMON/BIBLE STUDY

DATE: _____

PREACHER: _____

SCRIPTURE: _____

Key Verses:

Title: _____

Notes: _____

SERMON/BIBLE STUDY

Key Verses:

Reflections:

EMERGENCY SCRIPTURES (KJV)

† Abandonment .... Isaiah 41:10

† Anger .... Psalm 37:8-9

† Anxiety .... John 14:27

† Courage .... Joshua 1:9

† Criticism .... Luke 6:37

† Depression .... Psalm 34:17-18

† Doubt .... Matthew 21:21

† Encouragement .... John 16:33

† Failure .... Psalm 145:14-16

† Fear .... 2 Timothy 1:7

† Forgiveness .... Matthew 6:14-15

† Freedom .... John 8:31-36

⁻ Gladness .... Psalm 118:24

⁻ Gossip .... Matthew 12:37

⁻ Honesty .... Proverbs 11:1-3

⁻ Hope .... Romans 5:2

⁻ Jealousy .... James 3:16

⁻ Joy .... Psalm 16:11

⁻ Loneliness .... Deuteronomy 31:8

⁻ Peace .... John 14:27

⁻ Perseverance .... John 14:27

⁻ Sadness .... John 14:1

† Sorrow .... Matthew 5:4

† Stress .... Psalm 73:26

† Suffering .... 2 Corinthians 4:8-9

† Uncertainly .... Hebrews 10:23

† Worried .... Mathew 8:19-31

Thank you for supporting my small business.
I pray that this book brings you closer with your walk with the Lord.

www.ingramcontent.com/pod-product-compliance
Lightning Source LLC
Chambersburg PA
CBHW020238130626
46549CB00005B/1946